W9-CAW-697

READ WELL

Harriet Tubman

Teacher's Guide
Read Well 1 • Unit 26

U u

U says /uuu/.
Continuous Sound
Voiced (short)

Critical Foundations in Primary Reading

Marilyn Sprick, Lisa Howard, Ann Fidanque, Shelley V. Jones

ISBN 13-digit: 978-1-59318-449-0   ISBN 10-digit: 1-59318-449-2   131983/2-13

11 12 13 14 15   RRDHRBVA 17 16 15 14 13

Cambium
LEARNING®
Group | Voyager
LEARNING

Table of Contents
Unit 26
Harriet Tubman

How to Teach the Lessons (*continued*)

End of the Unit

I I Voiced (Word) **Unit A**	Mm /mmm/ **Monkey** Continuous Voiced **Unit B**	Ss /sss/ **Snake** Continuous Unvoiced **Unit 1**	Ee /eee/ **Emu** Continuous Voiced (Long) **Unit 2**	ee /eeee/ **Bee** Continuous Voiced (Long) **Unit 2**	Mm /mmm/ **Monkey** Continuous Voiced **Unit 3**
Aa /aaa/ **Ant** Continuous Voiced (Short) **Unit 4**	Dd /d/ **Dinosaur** Quick Voiced (not duh) **Unit 5**	th /ththth/ **the** Continuous Voiced **Unit 6**	Nn /nnn/ **Nest** Continuous Voiced **Unit 7**	Tt /t/ **Turkey** Quick Unvoiced (not tuh) **Unit 8**	Ww /www/ **Wind** Continuous Voiced (woo) **Unit 9**
Ii /iii/ **Insects** Continuous Voiced (Short) **Unit 10**	Th /Ththth/ **The** Continuous Voiced **Unit 10**	Hh /h/ **Hippo** Quick Unvoiced (not huh) **Unit 11**	Cc /c/ **Cat** Quick Unvoiced (not cuh) **Unit 12**	Rr /rrr/ **Rabbit** Continuous Voiced **Unit 13**	ea /eaeaea/ **Eagle** Continuous Voiced (Long) **Unit 13**
Sh/sh /shshsh/ **Sheep** Continuous Unvoiced **Unit 14**	Kk, -ck /k/ **Kangaroo** Quick Unvoiced (not kuh) **Unit 15**	oo /oooo/ **Moon** Continuous Voiced (Long) **Unit 16**	ar /ar/ **Shark** Voiced (R-Controlled) **Unit 17**	Wh/wh /wh/ **Whale** Quick Voiced **Unit 18**	Ee /ĕĕĕ/ **Engine or Ed** Continuous Voiced (Short) **Unit 19**
-y /-yyy/ **Fly** Continuous Voiced (Long) **Unit 20**	Ll /lll/ **Letter** Continuous Voiced **Unit 21**	Oo /ooo/ **Otter** Continuous Voiced (Short) **Unit 22**	Bb /b/ **Bat** Quick Voiced (not buh) **Unit 23**	all /all/ **Ball** Voiced **Unit 23**	Gg /g/ **Gorilla** Quick Voiced (not guh) **Unit 24**
Ff /fff/ **Frog** Continuous Unvoiced **Unit 25**	Uu /uuu/ **Umbrella** Continuous Voiced (Short) **Unit 26**	er /er/ **Sister** Voiced (R-Controlled) **Unit 27**	oo /oo/ **Book** Voiced (Short) **Unit 27**	Yy /y-/ **Yarn** Quick Voiced **Unit 28**	Aa /a/ **Ago** Voiced (Schwa) **Unit 28**
Pp /p/ **Pig** Quick Unvoiced (not puh) **Unit 29**	ay /ay/ **Hay** Voiced **Unit 29**	Vv /vvv/ **Volcano** Continuous Voiced **Unit 30**	Qu/qu /qu/ **Quake** Quick Unvoiced **Unit 31**	Jj /j/ **Jaguar** Quick Voiced (not juh) **Unit 32**	Xx /ksss/ **Fox** Continuous Unvoiced **Unit 33**
or /or/ **Horn** Voiced (R-Controlled) **Unit 33**	Zz /zzz/ **Zebra** Continuous Voiced **Unit 34**	a_e /a_e/ **Cake** Bossy E Voiced (Long) **Unit 34**	-y /-y/ **Baby** Voiced **Unit 35**	i_e /i_e/ **Kite** Bossy E Voiced (Long) **Unit 35**	ou /ou/ **Cloud** Voiced **Unit 36**
ow /ow/ **Cow** Voiced **Unit 36**	Ch/ch /ch/ **Chicken** Quick Unvoiced **Unit 37**	ai /ai/ **Rain** Voiced (Long) **Unit 37**	igh /igh/ **Flight** Voiced (Long) **Unit 38**	o_e /o_e/ **Bone** Bossy E Voiced (Long) **Unit 38**	ir /ir/ **Bird** Voiced (R-Controlled) **Unit 38**

Introduction
Harriet Tubman

Story Notes

Take a journey into American history. Explore slavery in the 1800s and the quest for freedom through the bravery and heroism of Harriet Tubman. Learn how Harriet Tubman followed the North Star to freedom, and then how she returned to the South to help others escape to the North.

Recommended Read Aloud

For reading outside of small group instruction

An Apple for Harriet Tubman by Glennette Tilley Turner

Biography

Introduce students to biographies with the story of Harriet Tubman. Students will identify with Harriet as a young child. What child wouldn't be tempted by juicy apples? How could you face being sold and taken away from your family? Students will learn about Harriet's escape to freedom and her heroic acts as the most famous conductor on the Underground Railroad.

Read Well Connection

Children will enjoy being able to read their own version of the Harriet Tubman story.

NOTE FROM THE AUTHORS

IMPRESSIONS

The story of Harriet Tubman has created spontaneous connections and lasting impressions with our young readers. A child in Texas exclaimed about an ancestor, "My mama said my grandma was a slave!"

In the act of reading about history, children seem to grow up with this unit. They recognize that they are reading passages of great importance. Even after several years have passed, children still recall the Harriet Tubman stories.

New and Important Objectives
A Research-Based Reading Program
Just Right for Young Children

Oral Language
Phonemic Awareness
Phonics
Fluency
Vocabulary
Comprehension

◆◆ Oral Language

In Units 21–38, language patterns are provided for high-frequency words and for some of the low-frequency words that are likely to require clarification. For English Language Learners and children with language delays, see page 10 for a list of the new high-frequency patterns.

Phonemic Awareness

Isolating Beginning, Middle, Ending Sounds, Segmenting, Blending, Rhyming, Onset and Rime

Phonics

Letter Sounds, Combinations, and Affixes

★ *Uu*
★ *-ed (/t/)*, ★ *un-*
Review • *Ss, Ee, ee, Mm, Aa, Dd, th, Nn, Tt, Ww, Ii, Th, Hh, Cc, Rr, ea, sh, Sh, Kk, -ck, oo, ar, wh, Wh, e (short), -y (as in "fly"), Ll, Oo, Bb, all, Gg, Ff*

Pattern Words

★ *ark,* ★ *asked,* ★ *asking,* ★ *asks,* ★ *Ben,* ★ *bubble gum,* ★ *but,* ★ *But,* ★ *crust,* ★ *cut,* ★ *dust,* ★ *farm,* ★ *farms,* ★ *feel,* ★ *Feel,* ★ *fun,* ★ *gust,* ★ *hundred,* ★ *logs,* ★ *must,* ★ *off,* ★ *resting,* ★ *rug,* ★ *run,* ★ *Run,* ★ *rust,* ★ *scrub,* ★ *sell,* ★ *shot,* ★ *sun,* ★ *telling,* ★ *tells,* ★ *things,* ★ *Tom,* ★ *umbrella,* ★ *unless,* ★ *unreal,* ★ *unselfish,* ★ *until,* ★ *us*

Review • *all, am, and, ask, at, At, bark, be, Be, began, Bell, can, can't, cart, creek, dark, did, didn't, dog, dogs, end, fast, free, Free, get, got, had, hard, he, He, hear, hid, Hid, hit, hog, hot, if, If, in, insects, it, It, kids, last, Last, Let, little, log, lot, man, Mark, me, mean, Meet, men, Men, met, moss, needed, not, on, On, ran, rest, rested, sang, see, See, sent, shark, she, She, sky, smell, star, Still, strong, ten, that, them, then, Then, thing, too, trees, wall, we, We, well, went, when, When, will, wind, with, With*

U says /uuu/.
Up, up umbrella,
/U/, /u/, /uuu/.

Continuous Sound

◆◆ = Oral language patterns   ★ = New in this unit

Phonics *(continued)*

Tricky Words

★*friend*, ★*Friend*, ★*friends*, ★*from*, ★*From*, ★*Harriet*, ★*worked*, ★*working*, ★*Working*

Review • *a, about, are, as, because, could, couldn't, do, eggs, go, I, is, Look, No, one, said, Said, should, so, So, the, The, there, to, two, want, Wants, wanted, was, what, where, Where, work, would*

Comprehension

Comprehension Strategies

Priming Background Knowledge, Making Connections, Predicting, Identifying, Describing, Defining, Explaining, Inferring, Responding, Questioning, Summarizing, Sequencing

Story Elements

Where (Setting), Who (Character), Want (Goal), What (Action)

Story Vocabulary

★Slave, ★Free, ★Brave, ★Moss, ★Cart

Text Structure

Beginning, Middle, End

Genre

Historical Fiction

Lessons

★Harriet Tubman was brave.

★Everyone wants to be free.

Written Response

Sentence Illustration, Sentence Completion, Sentence Writing, Sentence Comprehension—Multiple Choice, Summarizing—Story Map, Conventions—Beginning Capital, Period

Fluency

Accuracy, Expression, Phrasing, Rate

Daily Lesson Planning

PACING

Some students will begin the process of learning to read slowly but make rapid progress later. To be at grade level by the end of the year, most first graders need to complete Unit 30 by the end of the 27th week of school. Groups that are working at a slower pace may require more intensive *Read Well* instruction and practice. (See *Getting Started: A Guide to Implementation.*)

WEAK PASS CAUTION

If a student or students receive a Weak Pass on the previous two units, do not simply continue forward. See "Making Decisions" for Intervention Options.

ASSESSMENT

Upon completion of this unit, assess each student and proceed to Unit 27 as appropriate.

SAMPLE LESSON PLANS

The sample lesson plans illustrate how materials can be used for students with different learning needs. Each lesson plan is designed to provide daily decoding practice and story reading.

2-DAY PLAN • *Acceleration*

Day 1	**Day 2**
• Decoding Practice 1	• Decoding Practice 2
• Stories 1 and 2	• Stories 3 and 4
• Comprehension Work 1b*	• Comprehension Work 3*
• Comprehension Work 2*	• Comprehension Work 4*
• Homework 1, Story 2*	• Homework 2, Story 4*
	• Homework 3, Story 6*

In this 2-Day Plan, students skip Decoding Practice 3 and Stories 5 and 6. (Story 6 is included in the homework schedule.) Do not assign Comprehension Work 5a or 6a unless students have read the stories.

Important Note: Introduce the word "from" before students take home Story 6.

3-DAY PLAN

Day 1	**Day 2**	**Day 3**
• Decoding Practice 1	• Decoding Practice 2	• Decoding Practice 3
• Stories 1 and 2	• Stories 3 and 4	• Stories 5 and 6 and Summary
• Comprehension Work 1b*	• Comprehension Work 3*	• Comprehension Work 5a*
• Comprehension Work 2*	• Comprehension Work 4*	• Comprehension Work 6a*
• Homework 1, Story 2*	• Homework 2, Story 4*	• Homework 3, Story 6*
		• Homework 4, Storybook Decoding Review*

To avoid excessive seat-work, 2-, 3-, and 4-Day Plans omit or adjust use of Skill Work. If appropriate, Skill Work 1a, 5b, and 6b can be used anytime during or after this unit as independent work or homework.

4-DAY PLAN

Day 1	**Day 2**	**Day 3**	**Day 4**
• Decoding Practice 1	• Decoding Practice 2	• Decoding Practice 3	• Decoding Practice 4
• Stories 1 and 2	• Stories 3 and 4	• Stories 5 and 6 and Summary	• Review Stories 2, 4, and 6
• Comprehension Work 1b*	• Comprehension Work 3*	• Comprehension Work 5a*	• Comprehension Work 6a*
• Comprehension Work 2*	• Comprehension Work 4*	• Skill Work 5b* (Optional)	• Skill Work 6b* (Optional)
• Homework 1, Story 2*	• Homework 2, Story 4*	• Homework 3, Story 6*	• Homework 4, Storybook Decoding Review*

---

* From *Read Well* Comprehension and Skill Work (workbook), *Read Well* Homework (blackline masters), or Extra Practice in this book.

6-DAY PLAN • *Pre-Intervention*

Day 1
- Decoding Practice 1
- Story 1
- Skill Work 1a* (Optional)
- Comprehension Work 1b*

Day 2
- Review Decoding Practice 1
- Story 2
- Comprehension Work 2*
- Homework 1, Story 2*

Day 3
- Decoding Practice 2
- Story 3
- Comprehension Work 3*

Day 4
- Review Decoding Practice 2
- Story 4
- Comprehension Work 4*
- Homework 2, Story 4*

Day 5
- Decoding Practice 3
- Story 5
- Comprehension Work 5a*
- Skill Work 5b* (Optional)
- Homework 4, Storybook Decoding Review*

Day 6
- Decoding Practice 4
- Story 6 and Summary
- Comprehension Work 6a*
- Skill Work 6b* (Optional)
- Homework 3, Story 6*

PRE-INTERVENTION AND INTERVENTION

See *Getting Started: A Guide to Implementation* for information on how to achieve mastery at a faster pace with students who require six or more days of instruction.

8-DAY PLAN • *Intervention*

Day 1
- Decoding Practice 1
- Story 1
- Skill Work 1a* (Optional)
- Comprehension Work 1b*

Day 2
- Review Decoding Practice 1
- Story 2
- Comprehension Work 2*
- Homework 1, Story 2*

Day 3
- Decoding Practice 2
- Story 3
- Comprehension Work 3*

Day 4
- Review Decoding Practice 2
- Story 4
- Comprehension Work 4*
- Homework 2, Story 4*

Day 5
- Decoding Practice 3
- Story 5
- Comprehension Work 5a*
- Skill Work 5b* (Optional)
- Homework 4, Storybook Decoding Review*

Day 6
- Decoding Practice 4
- Story 6 and Summary
- Comprehension Work 6a*
- Skill Work 6b* (Optional)
- Homework 3, Story 6*

Day 7
- Extra Practice 1*
- Extra Practice 1 Fluency Passage*

Day 8
- Extra Practice 2*
- Extra Practice 2 Fluency Passages*

10-DAY PLAN • *Intervention*

Day 1
- Decoding Practice 1
- Story 1
- Skill Work 1a* (Optional)
- Comprehension Work 1b*

Day 2
- Review Decoding Practice 1
- Story 2
- Comprehension Work 2*
- Homework 1, Story 2*

Day 3
- Decoding Practice 2
- Story 3
- Comprehension Work 3*

Day 4
- Review Decoding Practice 2
- Story 4
- Comprehension Work 4*
- Homework 2, Story 4*

Day 5
- Decoding Practice 3
- Story 5
- Comprehension Work 5a*
- Skill Work 5b* (Optional)
- Homework 4, Storybook Decoding Review*

Day 6
- Decoding Practice 4
- Story 6 and Summary
- Comprehension Work 6a*
- Skill Work 6b* (Optional)
- Homework 3, Story 6*

Day 7
- Extra Practice 1*
- Extra Practice 1 Fluency Passage*

Day 8
- Extra Practice 2*
- Extra Practice 2 Fluency Passages*

Day 9
- Extra Practice 3*
- Extra Practice 3 Fluency Passage*

Day 10
- Extra Practice 4*
- Extra Practice 4 Fluency Passage*

Materials and Materials Preparation

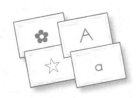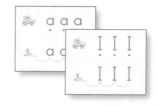

Core Lessons

Teacher Materials

READ WELL MATERIALS

- Unit 26 Teacher's Guide
- Sound and Word Cards for Units 1–26
- Game markers (optional for use with cover-up activities)
- *Assessment Manual* or page 54

SCHOOL SUPPLIES

- Stopwatch or watch with a second hand

Student Materials

READ WELL MATERIALS

- Decoding Book 3 for each student
- Unit 26 Storybook for each student
- Unit 26 Comprehension and Skill Work for each student (My Activity Book 3)
- Unit 26 Certificate of Achievement (blackline master page 55)
- Unit 26 Homework for each student (blackline masters)
  See *Getting Started* for suggested homework routines.

SCHOOL SUPPLIES

- Pencils, colors (optional—markers, crayons, or colored pencils)

Make one copy per student of each blackline master as appropriate for the group.

Note: For new or difficult Comprehension and Skill Work activities, make overhead transparencies from the blackline masters. Use the transparencies to demonstrate and guide practice.

Extra Practice Lessons

Note: Use these lessons only if needed.

Student Materials

READ WELL MATERIALS

- Unit 26 Extra Practice 1 and 2 for each student (blackline master pages 59 and 63)
- Unit 26 Extra Practice 1, 2, 3, and 4 Fluency Passages for each student (blackline master pages 60, 64, 66, and 68)
- Take-Home Game (blackline master page 61)

SCHOOL SUPPLIES

- Pencils, colors (markers, crayons, or colored pencils)
- White boards or paper

Important Tips

In this section, you will find:

Reading Widely—Exercising Patience

With the support of the Duet Stories, *Read Well* students are able to read sophisticated, decodable stories—even without complete letter-sound knowledge. Are they ready to read books that are not controlled?

Onset and Rime

Read Well's Accuracy and Fluency exercises provide children with practice in word pattern recognition.

Language and Vocabulary Practice—Review and High-Frequency Words

An additional focus on vocabulary and language skills often benefits English Language Learners and students with language delays.

Review the vocabulary words "rescue," "team," "habitat," and "mammal." Recursive use of vocabulary words provides students with an opportunity to deepen their conceptual knowledge.

A list of oral language patterns used with high-frequency words is also provided for additional emphasis and practice across settings.

Reading Widely
Exercising Patience

With each *Read Well* unit, students move further on the path to reading widely.

NATURAL READERS

By Unit 26, natural readers are often sounding out labels, reading directions, and enjoying their ability to read easy chapter books. When fidelity to *Read Well* is maintained, high-performing students are often reading books like the *Boxcar Children* and *Junie B. Jones* well before the end of first grade. Explicit instruction in *Read Well* allows high-performing students to learn quickly.

AVERAGE AND LOW-PERFORMING STUDENTS

By Unit 26, average and low-performing students are also well on their way to reading widely. But for these students, deviation into uncontrolled text can create confusion and decelerate learning. In this and upcoming units, students read sophisticated topics that include Harriet Tubman, Martin Luther King, volcanoes, and the rain forest. With these *Read Well* stories, children gain confidence and fluency. In uncontrolled text, students are forced to abandon sounding out.

To understand what happens when average and low-performing children try to read text with unknown letter-sound associations, try reading the following passage from H.G. Wells' *The War of the Worlds*. The passage has been adapted for your reading pleasure at 90% decodability.

CHAPTER 1: THE EVE OF THE WAR

No one would have believed in the last years of the nineteenth century that this world was being wa----d keenly and closely by in--------s greater than man's and yet as mortal as his own; that as men busied themselves about their v------s concerns they were scr--------- and studied, perhaps almost as narrowly as a man with a mi-------e might scr------e the tr-------t creatures that swarm and multiply in a drop of water. With infinite com-------y men went to and fro over this globe about their little affairs, s-----e in their ass------e of their em---e over matter.

Although much of the story's meaning can be deduced from the passage, the individual words take work to decipher. Even for proficient adult readers, reading with partial letter-sound knowledge detracts from the act of comprehension. Although the 96-word passage above may present an interesting challenge, it would be difficult to maintain attention through a longer passage or book. Imagine how difficult this must be for a young child with a shorter attention span.

Keep students focused on controlled practice and repeated readings of *Read Well* stories. Celebrate the themes, lessons, and language of the stories. Luckily, as they do with favorite bedtime stories, children can enjoy the same story over and over. Read widely *to* children, and soon your students will be able to read widely and well themselves.

Onset and Rime

Research Snapshot

After conducting a meta-analysis of 38 research studies that met a strict scientific criterion for inclusion, the National Reading Panel (2000) reported that "Findings provided solid support for the conclusion that systematic phonics instruction makes a bigger contribution to children's growth in reading than alternative programs providing unsystematic or no phonics instruction" (p. 2-85).

In addition, the panel found that effective programs included both synthetic phonics programs that emphasized blending of individual sounds and programs that emphasized blending of larger units (onsets and rimes). *Read Well* combines the teaching of synthetic phonics (Sounding Out Smoothly) with the teaching of onsets and rimes (Accuracy and Fluency).

PURPOSE

The Accuracy and Fluency Columns found in Decoding Practice provide systematic practice with onsets and rimes (word families). As reported by Adams (1990), Wylie and Durrell found that of 286 rimes found in primary grade texts (e.g., -ack, -ank, -eat, -ill), the vowels in 272 rimes were stable in every word in which they were found. Moreover, Wylie and Durrell reported that nearly 500 primary grade words could be derived from only 37 rimes. The Accuracy and Fluency Columns highlight the common rimes with underlining and provide ongoing practice to facilitate fluent recognition of common word patterns. Beginning with Unit 11 and the common rime "im" and "at," students have and will continue to regularly rehearse common patterns with review and newly introduced sounds.

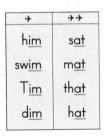

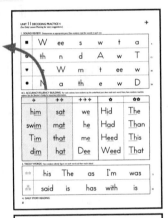

PROCEDURE

When teaching the Accuracy and Fluency Columns:

- For each column, have students say any underlined part, then read each word.
  Read the underlined part. (ell)
  Read the word. (well)

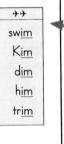

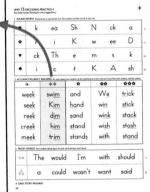

- Have students read the whole column.
  Read the whole column. (well, Bell, sell, smell)

- Repeat practice on each column, building accuracy first and then fluency.
  Read the whole column about this fast:
  well, Bell, sell . . . (well, Bell, sell, smell)

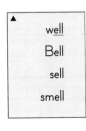

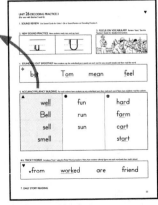

- Ask students what is the same about all the words.
  What can you tell me about "well," "Bell," "sell," and "smell"?
  (They rhyme. They all end in /ell/.)

Language and Vocabulary Practice
Review and High-Frequency Words

PURPOSE

The following lessons may be used to augment a structured oral language program. Periodic review is important to maintain knowledge and use of vocabulary words.

◆◆ FOR ENGLISH LANGUAGE LEARNERS AND CHILDREN WITH LANGUAGE DELAYS

REVIEW "RESCUE" AND "TEAM"

Review pictures of rescues.

- Help students review the word "rescue."
  You know the special word for saving people from danger.
  The word is . . . rescue.
- Have students identify the problem in a picture. Say something like:
  Look at the picture. What is the problem?
  (The people are in a burning house.)
- Have students help you use the word "rescuing" in a sentence.
  The firefighters are *saving* the people from the burning house.
  So we can say, the firefighters are . . . *rescuing* the people.
- Have students help you classify the rescuers as a team.
  The firefighters are working together so we also know they are a . . . *team*.

Repeat with other pictures of rescues.

REVIEW "HABITAT" AND "MAMMAL"

Review pictures of animals in their habitats.

- Help students review the word "habitat."
  The special word for an animal's special place on earth is . . . habitat.
  This otter lives in the sea, so we can say the sea is the otter's . . . habitat.
  Tell me about the otter's habitat. (The otter's habitat is the sea.)
- Have students help you classify the animal as a mammal.

Repeat with other pictures of animals in their habitats.

ORAL LANGUAGE PATTERNS USED WITH NEW HIGH-FREQUENCY WORDS

Sentences from *Read Well* Decoding Practice are repeated below for additional language practice.

ORAL LANGUAGE PATTERNS
★High-Frequency Words Introduced in This Unit
★ but – [Jonathan] wants to [play ball], *but* [it isn't time for recess].
★ cut – The man *cut* the tree down. What did the man do to the tree? (He *cut* it down.)
★ friend – [Tabitha] has a *friend*. What does [Tabitha] have? ([Tabitha] has a *friend*.)
★ Friends – *Friends* help each other. We are all . . . (*friends*).
★ from – Harriet ran away *from* the dogs. What did Harriet run away *from*? (She ran away *from* the dogs.)
★ must – [Javier] said, "I *must* [finish my work]." What did [Javier] say? (I *must* [finish my work].)
★ run – [Ming] can *run* fast. What can [Ming] do? ([Ming] can *run* fast.)
★ until – It won't get dark *until* the sun goes down.
★ us – [Mr. Z] will listen to *us* read. Who will [Mr. Z] listen to? ([He] will listen to *us*.)

How to Teach the Lessons

Teach from this section. Each instructional component is outlined in an easy-to-teach format. Special tips are provided to help you nurture student progress.

Decoding Practice 1

- Storybook Introduction
- Story 1, Duet
- Skill Work Activity 1a
- Comprehension Work Activity 1b
- Story 2, Solo
- Comprehension Work Activity 2

Decoding Practice 2

- Story 3, Duet
- Comprehension Work Activity 3
- Story 4, Solo
- Comprehension Work Activity 4

Decoding Practice 3

- Story 5, Duet
- Comprehension Work Activity 5a
- Skill Work Activity 5b
- Story 6, Solo
- Story Summary
- Comprehension Work Activity 6a
- Skill Work Activity 6b

Decoding Practice 4

Review Solo Stories

BUILDING INDEPENDENCE
Next Steps • Principles of Instruction

For Units 21–38, follow the scaffolded principles of instruction below.

Provide demonstration and/or guided practice only with:
- New sounds
- Pattern words with new sounds
- New Tricky Words
- New multisyllabic words

Provide independent practice (practice without your assistance or voice) on:
- New and review pattern words with known sounds
- Review Tricky Words
- Review multisyllabic words

If students make errors, provide appropriate corrections.
- Have students identify any difficult sound and then sound out the word. Provide discrimination practice.
- Reintroduce difficult Tricky Words based on the initial introduction procedures.

If students require your assistance on words with known sounds, evaluate placement and consider a Jell-Well Review.

① SOUND REVIEW

Use selected Sound Cards from Units 1–25.

② NEW SOUND INTRODUCTION

③ NEW SOUND PRACTICE

◆◆ **FOR ENGLISH LANGUAGE LEARNERS AND CHILDREN WITH LANGUAGE DELAYS**
Throughout Decoding Practice and Extra Practice, provide repeated use of the language patterns—both within and outside of lessons. See page 10 for tips.

◆◆ ④ SOUNDING OUT SMOOTHLY

- For each word, have students say the underlined part, sound out the word, and then read the word. Use the words in sentences as needed.
- Provide repeated practice. Mix group and individual turns, independent of your voice.

⑤ TRICKY WORDS

★ **New Tricky Word: "Harriet"**

Introduce the new word "Harriet." Say something like:

Your new Tricky Word is the name of the person we are going to read about.

Sound it out quietly to yourself. It's a Tricky Word so it won't sound out exactly right.

Say the name with me. Harriet

Read the name three times. (Harriet, Harriet, Harriet)

We're going to read about Harriet Tubman. Harriet is a very famous person who lived long ago.

⑥ ACCURACY AND FLUENCY BUILDING

★ **New word ending: /-ed/**

The Pencil Column introduces the /t/ sound for the word ending -ed. Until now, the -ed word ending has been used only in words where it is pronounced /ed/.

- For each column, have students say the underlined part, then read each word.
  After students read "ask-asking," say something like:

  The next word is a little tricky. It says "asked."

  The -ed in this word says /t/. We *asked* if we could read a story.

  Say the word "asked."

- Repeat process with "work-working-worked" in the Star Column.
- Repeat practice on each column, building accuracy first and then fluency.

⑦ DAILY STORY READING

Proceed to the Unit 26 Storybook. See Daily Lesson Planning for pacing suggestions.

⑧ COMPREHENSION AND SKILL WORK ACTIVITY I AND/OR ACTIVITY 2

See pages 20, 21, and/or 25.

UNIT **26** DECODING PRACTICE I
(For use with Stories 1 and 2)

I. SOUND REVIEW   Use Sound Cards for Units I–25.

2. NEW SOUND INTRODUCTION   Have students echo (repeat) the phrases. Do not have students read the poem.

U as in Umbrella
Capital letter U, small letter u,
U says uuu.
Up, up umbrella,
U, u, uuu.

3. NEW SOUND PRACTICE   Have students read, trace, and say /uuu/.

4. SOUNDING OUT SMOOTHLY   For each word, have students say the underlined part, then sound out the word and read it.

■ sun   fun   run

4. SOUNDING OUT SMOOTHLY (continued)

♥ but   cut   must   dust

● us   scrub   feel   free

★5. TRICKY WORDS   Introduce "Harriet" using the Tricky Word procedure.

★6. ACCURACY/FLUENCY BUILDING   For each column, have students say the underlined part, then read each word. Next have them read the column.

Tricky Word

★Harriet

Word Endings

resting
rested

ask
asking
★asked

work
working
worked

7. DAILY STORY READING

9

◆◆ **SENTENCE SUGGESTIONS**

■ run – [Ming] can *run* fast. What can [Ming] do?

♥ but – [Jonathan] wants to [play ball], *but* [it isn't time for recess].

♥ cut – The man *cut* the tree down. What did the man do to the tree?

♥ must – [Javier] said, "I *must* [finish my work]." What did [Javier] say?

♥ dust – When I clean, I always *dust* my furniture.

● us – [Mr. Z] will listen to *us* read. Who will [Mr. Z] listen to?

Sentence Suggestions: If a sentence is included, use it *after* decoding the individual word. The sentences may be used to build oral language patterns and vocabulary. Use of sentences also emphasizes that words have meaning.

❶ INTRODUCING THE STORYBOOK AND THE TITLE PAGE

Identifying—Title

Tell students this storybook is called *Let Freedom Ring*. There are two units in this storybook. Explain that this unit is about a real woman who lived long ago. This unit is called "Harriet Tubman."

Predicting

Ask students to look at the pictures to see if they can figure out what "Harriet Tubman" is going to be about.

❷ INTRODUCING VOCABULARY

Vocabulary—Slave, Free, Moss, Cart

Slave, Free

Put your finger under the first picture.

A *slave* was a person who was owned by another person and made to work hard.

Harriet Tubman was a slave.

If a person is a slave, he or she is not *free*.

A person who is free can live and work where he or she wants to.

Moss

Moss is a plant that grows on trees and rocks.

Cart

A *cart* is a wagon pulled by a horse.

Harriet Tubman

By Marilyn Sprick
Illustrated by Cedric Lucas

Vocabulary Words

slave	moss	cart
A slave was a person who was owned by another person and made to work hard. Harriet Tubman was a slave.	Moss is a plant that grows on trees and rocks.	A cart is a wagon pulled by a horse.

4   5

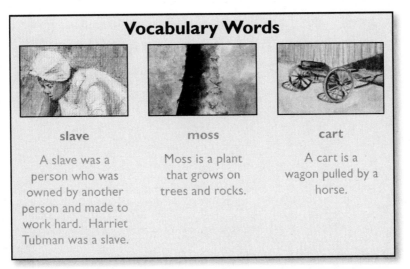

Vocabulary Words

slave	moss	cart
A slave was a person who was owned by another person and made to work hard. Harriet Tubman was a slave.	Moss is a plant that grows on trees and rocks.	A cart is a wagon pulled by a horse.

Defining Vocabulary—Slave, Moss, Cart

DUET STORY READING INSTRUCTIONS

Students read from their own storybooks.

The teacher reads the small text and students read the large text.

PACING

- 2- to 4-Day Plans: Have students do the first reading of Duet Story 1.

  Then proceed to repeated readings of Solo Story 2.

- 6- to 10-Day Plans: Have students do the first *and* second readings.

COMPREHENSION BUILDING:
DISCUSSION QUESTIONS AND TEACHER THINK ALOUDS

- Ask questions and discuss text on the first reading when indicated in the storybook in light gray text.

- Encourage students to answer questions with complete sentences when appropriate. Following a response, acknowledge the accuracy of the response and then say something like:

  I think this chapter will be about Harriet when she was little, too. Start your sentence with, "I think this chapter will be about . . ." (I think this chapter will be about Harriet when she was little.)

- If students have difficulty with a comprehension question, think aloud with them or reread the portion of the story that answers the question. Then, ask the question again.

PROCEDURES

1. First Reading

Have students choral read the student text.

2. Second Reading

Have students take turns, with each student reading one or two lines of student text.

STORY 1, DUET

work   working   worked

Follow the Star to Freedom

This story is about Harriet Tubman. What do you already know about Harriet?[1] I wonder why this story is called "Follow the Star to Freedom."[2]

CHAPTER 1

When Harriet Was Little

What do you think this chapter is about?[3]

Many years ago, thousands of black people were stolen from their homes in Africa. They were brought to the United States to be slaves. Slaves were owned by white people. Today, in the United States, no one can own another person. This story is about one slave—a real woman named Harriet Tubman.

When Harriet was little, she had to work. She had to work hard. Harriet could not rest. If she rested, she was hit. Harriet did not want to scrub, but she had to scrub. Harriet did not want to dust, but she had to dust.

FINGER TRACKING (Reminder)
Continue having children track the large text with their fingers.

6

❶ **Priming Background Knowledge**
❷ **Teacher Think Aloud—Questioning**
❸ **Predicting**

Teacher Think Aloud
Treat this topic with sensitivity. After students have answered the questions at the bottom of the page, say something like: Today, all children get to go to school. They get to play and they help out at home. Harriet's life was different because she was a slave. She didn't get to go to school or play. Instead, she had to work every day and all day for the people who owned her.

Look at the picture. What is Harriet doing?**1** What kind of jobs did Harriet have to do when she was little?**2**

7

❶ **Identifying—Action** (She is cleaning house.)
❷ **Identifying—What** (She had to dust and scrub.)

Harriet asked if she could work with the men. Harriet said, "I am strong. I can cut logs." Harriet worked with the men. She worked hard, but she wanted to be free.

At the end of this chapter, Harriet was older. Tell me two facts about Harriet.[1]

8

❶ **Explaining, Describing** (Harriet was a slave. She liked working outside. She cut logs. She was strong. She wanted to be free . . .)

SOUND PAGE

Use work pages from the workbook.

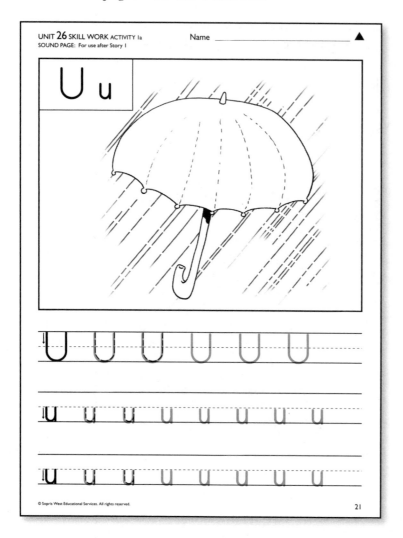

UNIT **26** SKILL WORK ACTIVITY 1a
SOUND PAGE: For use after Story 1

Name _____

CHECKOUT OPPORTUNITY

While students are working on Comprehension and Skill Work, you may wish to listen to individuals read a Decoding Practice or Solo Story. If the student makes an error, gently correct and have the student reread the column, row, or sentence.

PROCEDURES

For each step, demonstrate and guide practice as needed.

1. Handwriting—Basic Instructions

- Have students identify the capital letter U as in "Umbrella."
- Have students trace and write the capital letter U—leaving a finger space between each letter. Repeat with the small letter u on the last rows.
- In each row have students circle their best letter.

2. Coloring—Basic Instructions

Have students color the picture of the umbrella, using at least three colors.

Note: Neat work helps students take pride in their efforts.

STORY COMPREHENSION

Use work pages from the workbook.

Writing
Identifying—Who

Identifying—Action

Identifying—What

Writing
Identifying—Goal
Conventions—Beginning Capital, Period

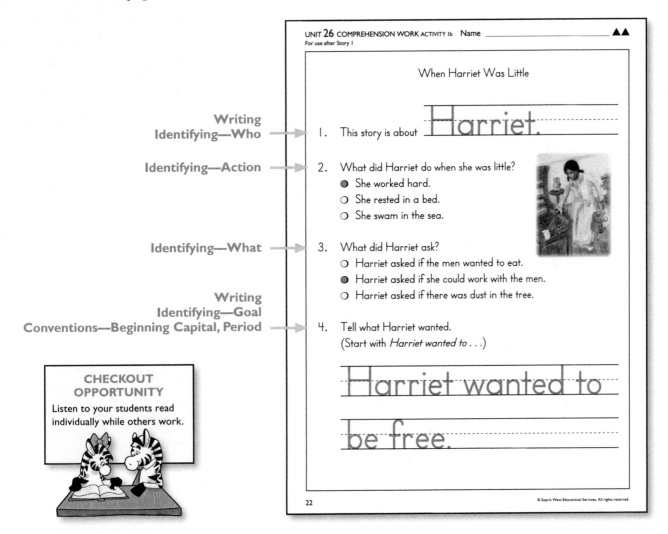

UNIT **26** COMPREHENSION WORK ACTIVITY Ib   Name _____   ▲▲
For use after Story I

When Harriet Was Little

1. This story is about <u>Harriet.</u>

2. What did Harriet do when she was little?
   - ● She worked hard.
   - ○ She rested in a bed.
   - ○ She swam in the sea.

3. What did Harriet ask?
   - ○ Harriet asked if the men wanted to eat.
   - ● Harriet asked if she could work with the men.
   - ○ Harriet asked if there was dust in the tree.

4. Tell what Harriet wanted.
   (Start with *Harriet wanted to . . .*)

   <u>Harriet wanted to</u>

   <u>be free.</u>

22   © Sopris West Educational Services. All rights reserved.

CHECKOUT OPPORTUNITY

Listen to your students read individually while others work.

PROCEDURES

For each step, demonstrate and guide practice as needed.

- (Demonstrate) Have students orally respond to items while you demonstrate how to complete the page.
- (Guide) Have students orally respond to the items, but do not demonstrate how to complete the page.
- (Independent With Support) Have students silently read over the items and ask any questions they may have.

1. Sentence Completion—Basic Instructions (Item 1)

Have students read and complete the sentence, and end it with a period.

2. Multiple Choice—Basic Instructions (Items 2, 3)

Have students fill in the bubble for the correct answer. Periodically, think aloud with students. Discuss the multiple choice options. As appropriate, ask questions like: "Does the first answer make sense?" "Is that what the book said?" "Is the answer completely correct?"

3. Sentence Writing—Basic Instructions (Item 4)

- Have students read the direction and brainstorm possible responses using complete sentences.
- Have students write complete sentences that start with a capital letter and end with a period.

SOLO STORY READING INSTRUCTIONS

Students read from their own storybooks.

COMPREHENSION BUILDING:
DISCUSSION QUESTIONS AND TEACHER THINK ALOUDS

- Ask questions and discuss text on the first reading when indicated in the storybook in light gray text.
- Encourage students to answer questions with complete sentences when appropriate.
- If students have difficulty with a comprehension question, think aloud with them or reread the portion of the story that answers the question. Then, ask the question again.

PROCEDURES

1. First Reading

- Mix group and individual turns on student-read sentences. On individual turns, gently correct any error, and then have the student reread the text.
- After students complete the first reading and before the second reading, have students practice a paragraph. First demonstrate expressive reading for students, then give individual turns. Acknowledge student efforts.

2. Second Reading

- Mix group and individual turns, independent of your voice.
  Have students work toward an accuracy goal of 0–2 errors.
  Quietly keep track of errors made by all students in each group.
- After reading the story, practice any difficult words.
- If the group has not reached the accuracy goal, have the group reread the story, mixing group and individual turns.

3. Repeated Readings
a. Timed Readings

- Once the accuracy goal has been achieved, have individual students read the page while the other children track the text with their fingers and whisper read. Time individuals for 30 seconds and encourage each student to work for a personal best.
- Count the number of words read correctly in 30 seconds (words read minus errors). Multiply by two to determine words correct per minute. Record student scores.

Note: Accuracy should precede rate. If a student is unable to read with close to 100% accuracy, do not time the student. The personal goal should be accuracy. If the student is unable to read with accuracy, evaluate group placement and consider a Jell-Well Review.

b. Partner Reading

During students' daily independent work, have them do Partner Reading.

c. Homework 1

Have students read the story at home. (A reprint of this story is available on a blackline master in *Read Well* Homework.)

---

sun   run   **fun**

CHAPTER 2

Working With the Men

Harriet didn't want to scrub because she wanted to work with the men. Harriet didn't want to dust because she wanted to work in the sun. She wanted to see the sky.

Harriet was strong, so she got to cut logs. She worked hard with the men. She could see the sky and feel the wind. Still, Harriet wanted to be free. So, Harriet sang as she worked, "Let us go. Let us be free."

Why did Harriet want to work with the men?**1** What did Harriet do as she worked?**2**What did Harriet want more than anything?**3**

9

❶ **Explaining** (She wanted to work in the sun. She wanted to see the sky.)

❷ **Identifying—Action** (She sang.)

❸ **Identifying—Goal** (She wanted to be free.)

10

SENTENCE COMPREHENSION

Use work pages from the workbook.

Illustrating—Setting, Action

Writing,
Identifying—Action
Conventions—Beginning Capital, Period

UNIT **26** COMPREHENSION WORK ACTIVITY 2   Name _____ ■
For use after Story 2

Working With the Men

Sentence Illustration

Harriet wanted to work in the sun. So she worked with the men.
She cut logs.

Answering Questions With Sentence Writing

What did Harriet do as she worked?
(Start with *Harriet . . .*)

Harriet sang.
(or "Harriet would sing.")

© Sopris West Educational Services. All rights reserved.   23

CHECKOUT OPPORTUNITY
Listen to your students read individually while others work.

PROCEDURES

For each step, demonstrate and guide practice as needed.

1. Sentence Illustration—Specific Instructions
- Have students read the sentences about Harriet working.
- Then, have them draw a picture of Harriet working.

2. Sentence Writing—Basic Instructions
- Have students read the question and brainstorm possible responses using complete sentences.
- Have students write complete sentences that start with a capital letter and end with a period.

❶ SOUND REVIEW

Use selected Sound Cards from Units 1–26, or the Sound Review on Decoding Practice 4.

❷ NEW SOUND PRACTICE

◆◆ **❸ FOCUS ON VOCABULARY**

★ **New vocabulary word: "slave"**

Introduce the word "slave" and give examples of its meaning. Say something like:

Your new vocabulary word is "slave." Tell me your new word. (slave)

Long ago, some people thought they could own people who worked for them.

A *slave* was someone who was owned by another person and made to work hard.

Someone who was owned by another person and made to work hard was called a . . . (slave).

A slave was not free. A slave could not even go to school.

❹ SOUNDING OUT SMOOTHLY

- For each word, have students say the underlined part, sound out the word, and then read the word. Use the words in sentences as needed.
- Provide repeated practice. Mix group and individual turns, independent of your voice.

◆◆ **❺ ACCURACY AND FLUENCY BUILDING**

- For each column, have students say any underlined part, then read each word.
- Have students read the whole column.
- Repeat practice on each column, building accuracy first and then fluency.

Note: Once students are accurate on the Square Column, give individual turns. Have students try to read the column in five seconds or less.

◆◆ **❻ TRICKY WORDS**

★ **New Tricky Word: "friends"**

To introduce the new Tricky Word "friends," you may wish to use the following variation of the standard format. Write "fri<u>ends</u>" on the chalkboard.

- Ask students what small word they see in their Tricky Word ("ends").
- Next, cross out the silent <u>i</u> in the word.
- Have students sound out the word.
- Provide repeated practice. Mix group and individual turns, independent of your voice.

❼ DAILY STORY READING

Proceed to the Unit 26 Storybook. See Daily Lesson Planning for pacing suggestions.

❽ COMPREHENSION AND SKILL WORK ACTIVITY 3 AND/OR ACTIVITY 4

See pages 31 and/or 35.

◆◆ For ELLs and children with language delays, provide repeated and extended practice with the language patterns. See page 10 for tips.

UNIT **26** DECODING PRACTICE 2
(For use with Stories 3 and 4)

1. SOUND REVIEW Use Sound Cards for Units 1–26 or Sound Review on Decoding Practice 4.

2. NEW SOUND PRACTICE Have students read, trace, and say /uuu/.

★3. FOCUS ON VOCABULARY Introduce "slave." See the Teacher's Guide for detailed instructions.

4. SOUNDING OUT SMOOTHLY For each word, have students say the underlined part, sound out the word in one smooth breath, and then read the word.

● b<u>u</u>t   f<u>ar</u>ms   m<u>o</u>ss   m<u>u</u>st

5. ACCURACY/FLUENCY BUILDING For each column, have students say any underlined part, then read each word. Next, have students read the column.

▲	■	☆
t<u>e</u>n	<u>u</u>ntil	<u>a</u>sks
B<u>e</u>n	<u>u</u>nless	<u>a</u>sking
thing	<u>u</u>nreal	te<u>ll</u>s
things		te<u>ll</u>ing

REPEATED PRACTICE

Practice each column and row more than once by mixing group and individual turns.

★6. TRICKY WORDS Introduce "friends" using the Tricky Word procedure. Next, have students silently figure out each word and then read it aloud.

♥ ★friends   about   work   because

◆◆ SENTENCE SUGGESTIONS

● moss – *Moss* is a plant that grows on trees or rocks.

■ until – It won't get dark *until* the sun goes down.

♥ friends – *Friends* help each other. We are all . . . (*friends*).

7. DAILY STORY READING

10

Sentence Suggestions: Use the appropriate suggested sentence *after* decoding each individual word.

DUET STORY READING INSTRUCTIONS

Students read from their own storybooks.
The teacher reads the small text and students read the large text.

PACING

- 2- to 4-Day Plans: Have students do the first reading of Duet Story 3.
  Then, proceed to repeated readings of Solo Story 4.
- 6- to 10-Day Plans: Have students do the first *and* second readings.

COMPREHENSION BUILDING:
DISCUSSION QUESTIONS AND TEACHER THINK ALOUDS

- Ask questions and discuss text on the first reading when indicated in the storybook in light gray text.
- Encourage students to answer questions with complete sentences when appropriate.
- If students have difficulty with a comprehension question, think aloud with them or reread the portion of the story that answers the question. Then, ask the question again.

PROCEDURES

1. **First Reading**

   Mix group and individual turns on student-read sentences. On individual turns, gently correct any error, and then have the student reread the text.

2. **Second Reading**

   Repeat the reading only as needed for comprehension.

log   dog   hog

CHAPTER 3

Harriet Wants to Be Free

Harriet Tubman lived in the South. Some black people were freed by their owners, but Harriet knew that she would never be free unless she ran away. She would have to go to the North where black people were free. Harriet's father, Ben, knew that Harriet dreamed of being free.

Ben began telling Harriet things. Ben said, "Harriet, see that star in the sky. It tells us where to go."

Harriet said, "I see the star. But what if it is too dark? If I can't see the star, what should I do?"

Ben said, "Feel the moss on the trees."

Ben explained, "Moss only grows on the north side of trees. To get to the North, just follow the moss."

Who was Ben?[1] Harriet wanted to run to freedom. Ben told her two things that would help her find her way to the North.[2] What were they?[3]

11

❶ **Identifying—Who** (Ben was Harriet's father.)

❷ **Teacher Think Aloud**

❸ **Explaining** (Harriet could follow the star. She could feel the moss on the trees.)

One day, Harriet knew it was time to go. She would follow the moss. She would follow the star.

Harriet went in the dark. She ran to the trees. She wanted to be free. It was hard, but Harriet could feel the moss and see the star.

STORY 3, DUET

EXPLAINING
Teacher Think Aloud
Harriet couldn't follow the star, but her father had told her to follow the moss growing on the trees. Look at my picture. It's a little hard to tell, but there is moss growing on each tree, but only on the north side of each tree. Harriet knew that if she followed the moss, she would be traveling north.

At the end of the chapter, what did Harriet do?[1]

12

❶ **Inferring, Explaining** (She ran away.)

STORY COMPREHENSION

Use work pages from the workbook.

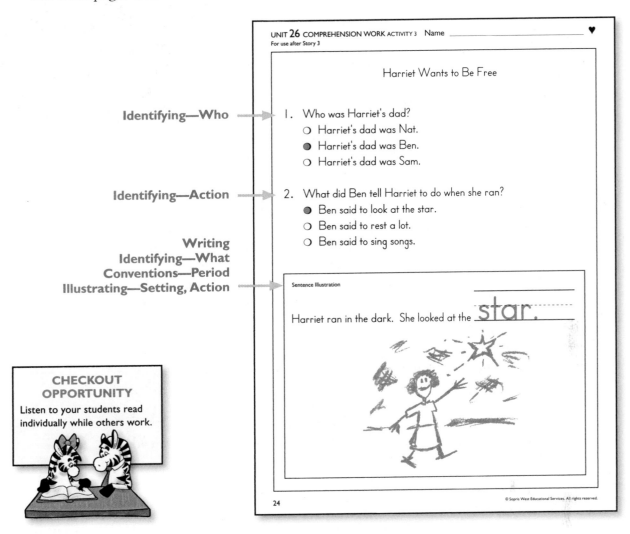

Identifying—Who

Identifying—Action

Writing
Identifying—What
Conventions—Period
Illustrating—Setting, Action

CHECKOUT OPPORTUNITY

Listen to your students read individually while others work.

UNIT **26** COMPREHENSION WORK ACTIVITY 3   Name _____
For use after Story 3

Harriet Wants to Be Free

1. Who was Harriet's dad?
   ○ Harriet's dad was Nat.
   ● Harriet's dad was Ben.
   ○ Harriet's dad was Sam.

2. What did Ben tell Harriet to do when she ran?
   ● Ben said to look at the star.
   ○ Ben said to rest a lot.
   ○ Ben said to sing songs.

Sentence Illustration

Harriet ran in the dark. She looked at the star.

24

PROCEDURES

For each step, demonstrate and guide practice as needed.

1. Multiple Choice—Basic Instructions (Items 1, 2)

Have students fill in the bubble for the correct answer. Periodically, think aloud with students. Discuss the multiple choice options. As appropriate, ask questions like: "Does the first answer make sense?" "Is that what the book said?" "Is the answer completely correct?"

2. Sentence Illustration—Basic Instructions

Have students read the sentence, complete it, and then complete the illustration.

SOLO STORY READING INSTRUCTIONS
Students read from their own storybooks.

COMPREHENSION BUILDING:
DISCUSSION QUESTIONS AND TEACHER THINK ALOUDS

- Ask questions and discuss text on the first reading when indicated in the storybook in light gray text.
- Encourage students to answer questions with complete sentences when appropriate.
- If students have difficulty with a comprehension question, think aloud with them or reread the portion of the story that answers the question. Then, ask the question again.

PROCEDURES

1. First Reading

- Mix group and individual turns on student-read sentences. On individual turns, gently correct any error, and then have the student reread the text.
- After students complete the first reading and before the second reading, have students practice a paragraph. First demonstrate expressive reading for students, then give individual turns. Acknowledge student efforts.

2. Second Reading

- Mix group and individual turns, independent of your voice.
  Have students work toward an accuracy goal of 0–2 errors.
  Quietly keep track of errors made by all students in each group.
- After reading the story, practice any difficult words.
- If the group has not reached the accuracy goal, have the group reread the story, mixing group and individual turns.

3. Repeated Readings

a. Timed Readings

- Once the accuracy goal has been achieved, have individual students read the page while the other children track the text with their fingers and whisper read.
  Time individuals for 30 seconds and encourage each student to work for a personal best.
- Count the number of words read correctly in 30 seconds (words read minus errors). Multiply by two to determine words correct per minute. Record student scores.

b. Partner Reading

During students' daily independent work, have them do Partner Reading.

c. Homework 2

Have students read the story at home. (A reprint of this story is available on a blackline master in *Read Well* Homework.)

CHAPTER 4

On the Run

At the end of the last chapter, Harriet ran away.**1** What do you think happened to her?**2**

Harriet said, "I must be free. I must."

The men sent dogs to get Harriet, but she ran. The dogs could smell Harriet, but Harriet ran in the creek. Then the dogs couldn't smell Harriet. Harriet said, "I must be free. I must."

Harriet ran in the dark. She hid on farms. She hid with friends. Harriet ran and ran until she was free. Then Harriet sang, "I am free. See me. I am free at last."

How did Harriet get away from the dogs?**3** While she ran for freedom, Harriet had to hide. Where did she hide?**4** What happened at the end of this chapter?**5**

13

1 **Teacher Think Aloud—Summarizing**

2 **Predicting**

3 **Explaining** (She ran in the creek so they couldn't smell her.)

4 **Identifying—Where** (Harriet hid on farms and with friends.)

5 **Explaining** (Harriet ran until she was free.)

STORY 4, SOLO

14

STORY MAP

Use work pages from the workbook.

Summarizing, Sequencing
Conventions—Period

Explaining—Beginning
Identifying—Who

Identifying—Who

Identifying—Goal

Explaining—Middle
Identifying—Where

Explaining—End

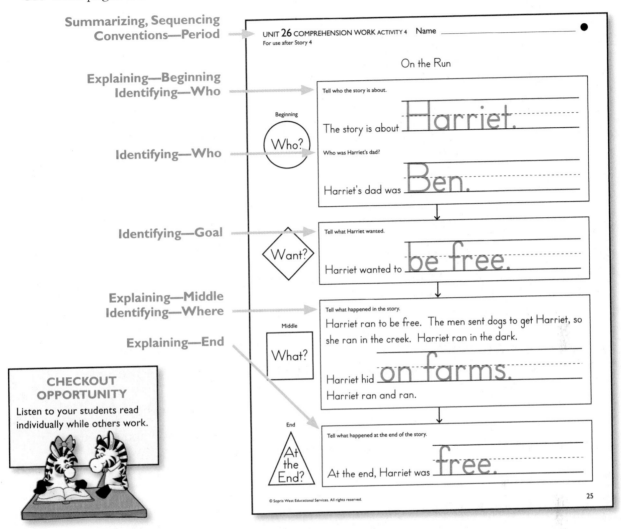

UNIT **26** COMPREHENSION WORK ACTIVITY 4   Name _____

For use after Story 4

On the Run

Beginning

Who?

Tell who the story is about.

The story is about ___Harriet.

Who was Harriet's dad?

Harriet's dad was ___Ben.

Want?

Tell what Harriet wanted.

Harriet wanted to ___be free.

Middle

What?

Tell what happened in the story.

Harriet ran to be free. The men sent dogs to get Harriet, so she ran in the creek. Harriet ran in the dark.

Harriet hid ___on farms.

Harriet ran and ran.

End

At the End?

Tell what happened at the end of the story.

At the end, Harriet was ___free.

25

CHECKOUT OPPORTUNITY

Listen to your students read individually while others work.

Story Map—Basic Instructions

- Using a blank or overhead copy of the story map, help students identify the basic story elements—who the story is about, what happened in the story, what the problem was, and what happened at the end.
- Have students fill in the blanks to create a story map.
- Remind students that a story map helps them retell or summarize the important parts of a story.

Note: You may wish to remind students that a sentence ends with a period.

➊ SOUND REVIEW

➋ NEW SOUND PRACTICE

◆◆ **➌ FOCUS ON VOCABULARY**

Review vocabulary word: "slave"

Have students review the word "slave" and use it in a sentence.

Say something like:

Someone who was owned by another person and made to work hard was called a . . . (*slave*).

Was a slave someone who could go to school? (No)

Was a slave someone who was free? (No)

[Christopher], tell me something about a slave.

Start with "A slave was someone who . . . "

(A slave was someone who [was owned by another person].)

[Hailey], tell me something about a slave. (A slave was someone who . . .)

➍ SOUNDING OUT SMOOTHLY

- For each word, have students say the underlined part, sound out the word, and then read the word. Use the words in sentences as needed.
- Provide repeated practice. Mix group and individual turns, independent of your voice.

➎ ACCURACY AND FLUENCY BUILDING

- For each column, have students say any underlined part, then read each word.
- Have students read the whole column.
- Repeat practice on each column, building accuracy first and then fluency.

Note: After students have read each column, ask them what is the same about all the words in that column (e.g., "well", "Bell," "sell," and "smell" rhyme).

◆◆ **➏ TRICKY WORDS**

★ **New Tricky Word: "from"**

Use the standard Tricky Word format to introduce the new word "from."

➐ DAILY STORY READING

Proceed to the Unit 26 Storybook. See Daily Lesson Planning for pacing suggestions.

➑ COMPREHENSION AND SKILL WORK ACTIVITY 5 AND/OR ACTIVITY 6

See pages 42, 43 and/or 48, 49.

◆◆ For ELLs and children with language delays, provide repeated and extended practice with the language patterns. See page 10 for tips.

UNIT **26** DECODING PRACTICE 3
(For use with Stories 5 and 6)

1. SOUND REVIEW Use Sound Cards for Units 1–26 or Sound Review on Decoding Practice 4.

2. NEW SOUND PRACTICE Have students read, trace, and say /uuu/.

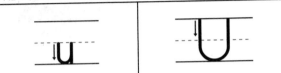

3. FOCUS ON VOCABULARY Review "slave." See the Teacher's Guide for detailed instructions.

4. SOUNDING OUT SMOOTHLY Have students say the underlined part, sound out each word in one smooth breath, and then read the word.

but   T<u>om</u>   m<u>ea</u>n   <u>f</u>eel

5. ACCURACY/FLUENCY BUILDING For each column, have students say any underlined part, then read each word. Next, have students read the column.

▲	●	✿
w<u>ell</u>	fun	<u>h</u>ard
Bell	run	f<u>ar</u>m
sell	sun	<u>c</u>art
smell		st<u>ar</u>t

★6. TRICKY WORDS Introduce "from" using the Tricky Word procedure. Next, have students silently figure out each word and then read it aloud.

♥ ★from   <u>worked</u>   are   friend

7. DAILY STORY READING

11

Sentence Suggestions: Use the appropriate suggested sentence *after* decoding each individual word.

DUET STORY READING INSTRUCTIONS

Students read from their own storybooks.

The teacher reads the small text and students read the large text.

PACING

- 3- to 4-Day Plans: Have students do the first reading of Duet Story 5.

  Then proceed to repeated readings of Solo Story 6.
- 6- to 10-Day Plans: Have students do the first *and* second readings as needed.

COMPREHENSION BUILDING: DISCUSSION QUESTIONS AND TEACHER THINK ALOUDS

- Ask questions and discuss text on the first reading when indicated in the storybook in light gray text.
- Encourage students to answer questions with complete sentences when appropriate.
- If students have difficulty with a comprehension question, think aloud with them or reread the portion of the story that answers the question. Then, ask the question again.

PROCEDURES

1. Summarizing and Inferring

Have students review who and what the story is about.

Say something like:

This is Chapter 5 of "Harriet Tubman." Who is the main character? (Harriet Tubman)

Who was Harriet Tubman? (She was a slave.)

What did Harriet Tubman do? (She ran away and escaped to the North.)

2. First Reading

- Tell students they are going to read the next chapter about Harriet Tubman.
- Have students choral read the student text.

3. Second Reading

Have students take turns, with each student reading one line of student text.

---
from   friend

CHAPTER 5

From Friend to Friend

Harriet Tubman was a slave who escaped to the North. She traveled along the Underground Railroad. The Underground Railroad wasn't really a railroad. It was a way to freedom. Each stop was the house of someone who wanted to help the slaves escape. When Harriet was free, she joined the Underground Railroad and began to help others escape to freedom. Once Harriet was free, what did she do?❶

Harriet was free, but Tom was not.

The sun was hot, and Tom worked hard.

Still, the man was mean. He would hit Tom.

Tom wanted to be free.

15

❶ **Identifying—What** (She helped other slaves run to freedom.)

Tom and Bell had kids. Bell said to Tom, "I do not want the man to sell the kids."

Tom said, "Then we must run from the man."

What did Bell tell Tom?**1** Who wanted to be free in this story?**2**

16

❶ Identifying—What (Bell said that she didn't want the man to sell the kids.)

❷ Identifying—Who (Tom and Bell wanted to be free.)

Tom met with Harriet. It would be hard with all the kids, but Harriet said, "Meet me when it is dark."

Why did Harriet think it would be hard for Tom and Bell to escape?**1**

Harriet hid them in a cart. She hid them in the trees. Harriet, Tom, Bell, and the kids ran.

Where did Harriet hide Tom and Bell and their kids?**2** I think it was very hard to escape.**3** How do you think the kids felt?**4**

It was a hard journey, but Harriet showed Tom, Bell, and their children how to follow the North Star. They followed the star and ran from friend to friend along the Underground Railroad.

Do you think Harriet, Bell, Tom, and the children made it to freedom?**5**

17

DESCRIBING, FOCUS ON VOCABULARY— BRAVE

After completing the page, say something like: Harriet Tubman was very *brave* when she ran away to the north. Was she brave when she helped Tom and his family? (Yes) Yes, she was in danger of getting caught again, but she helped Tom and has family anyway. Tell me about Harriet Tubman, using the word "brave."

Who else was brave in this chapter?

❶ **Inferring, Explaining** (It would be hard to run and hide with young children.)

❷ **Identifying—Where** (They hid in a cart, in trees, and with friends.)

❸ **Teacher Think Aloud**

❹ **Inferring**

❺ **Predicting**

STORY COMPREHENSION

Use work pages from the workbook.

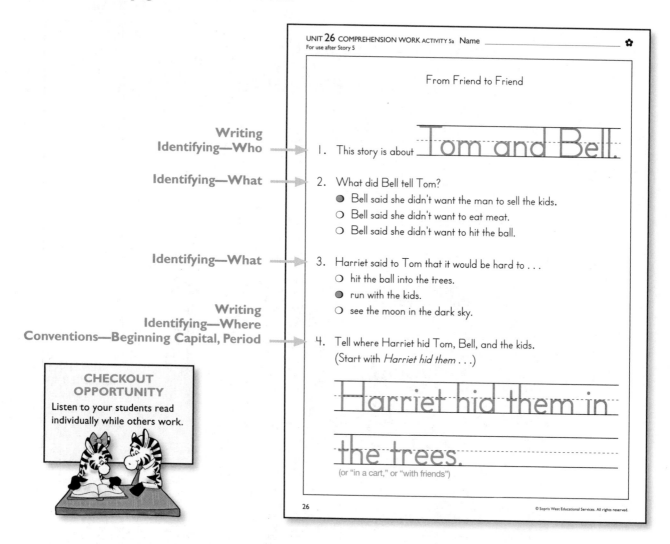

**Writing
Identifying—Who** →

Identifying—What →

Identifying—What →

**Writing
Identifying—Where
Conventions—Beginning Capital, Period** →

UNIT **26** COMPREHENSION WORK ACTIVITY 5a Name _____
For use after Story 5

From Friend to Friend

1. This story is about __Tom and Bell.__

2. What did Bell tell Tom?
   - ● Bell said she didn't want the man to sell the kids.
   - ○ Bell said she didn't want to eat meat.
   - ○ Bell said she didn't want to hit the ball.

3. Harriet said to Tom that it would be hard to . . .
   - ○ hit the ball into the trees.
   - ● run with the kids.
   - ○ see the moon in the dark sky.

4. Tell where Harriet hid Tom, Bell, and the kids.
   (Start with *Harriet hid them* . . .)

   __Harriet hid them in__

   __the trees.__
   (or "in a cart," or "with friends")

26

CHECKOUT OPPORTUNITY

Listen to your students read individually while others work.

PROCEDURES

For each step, demonstrate and guide practice as needed.

1. **Sentence Completion—Basic Instructions** (Item 1)

   Have students read and complete the sentence, and end it with a period.

2. **Multiple Choice—Basic Instructions** (Items 2, 3)

   Have students fill in the bubble for the correct answer. Periodically, think aloud with students. Discuss the multiple choice options. As appropriate, ask questions like: "Does the first answer make sense?" "Is that what the book said?" "Is the answer completely correct?"

3. **Sentence Writing—Basic Instructions** (Item 4)

   - Have students read the direction and brainstorm possible responses using complete sentences.
   - Have students write complete sentences that start with a capital letter and end with a period.

ALPHABET DETECTIVE

Use work pages from the workbook.

CHECKOUT OPPORTUNITY

Listen to your students read individually while others work.

UNIT **26** SKILL WORK ACTIVITY 5b
ALPHABET DETECTIVE: For use after Story 5

Name _____

U as in Umbrella

Capital letter U, small letter u.

U says uuu.

Up, up umbrella,

U, u, uuu.

27

PROCEDURES

For each step, demonstrate and guide practice as needed.

1. **Letter Find—Basic Instructions**

   • Have students look at the first box at the top of the page and follow the directions. Ask:

   What letters will you look for? (The capital letter U and the small letter u)

   What will you do when you find a capital letter U or a small letter u? (Draw a triangle around it.)

   • Have students look at the second box at the top of the page. Ask:

   What other letter will you look for? (The small letter b)

   What will you do when you find a small letter b? (Draw a circle around it.)

2. **Self-Monitoring—Basic Instructions**

   Have students systematically check each line after finishing the task.

   Alternative: At the beginning of the exercise, tell students the number of u's they will draw a triangle around, and the number of b's they will circle. Have students write the numbers on the top of their paper. When students complete the activity, have them count the number of triangles and circles they have drawn. If the numbers are incorrect, they can recheck each line.

3. **Coloring—Optional**

   Have students carefully color the picture, using at least three colors.

   Note: If students have difficulty with the multi-step directions, have them do just the first step.

SOLO STORY READING INSTRUCTIONS

Students read from their own storybooks.

COMPREHENSION BUILDING:
DISCUSSION QUESTIONS AND TEACHER THINK ALOUDS

- Ask questions and discuss text on the first reading when indicated in the storybook in light gray text.
- Encourage students to answer questions with complete sentences when appropriate.
- If students have difficulty with a comprehension question, think aloud with them or reread the portion of the story that answers the question. Then, ask the question again.

PROCEDURES

1. First Reading

- Mix group and individual turns on student-read sentences. On individual turns, gently correct any error, and then have the student reread the text.
- After students complete the first reading and before the second reading, have students practice a paragraph. First demonstrate expressive reading for students, then give individual turns. Acknowledge student efforts.

2. Second Reading

- Mix group and individual turns, independent of your voice.
  Have students work toward an accuracy goal of 0–2 errors.
  Quietly keep track of errors made by all students in each group.
- After reading the story, practice any difficult words.
- If the group has not reached the accuracy goal, have the group reread the story, mixing group and individual turns.

3. Repeated Readings
a. Timed Readings

- Once the accuracy goal has been achieved, have individual students read the page while the other children track the text with their fingers and whisper read.
  Time individuals for 30 seconds and encourage each student to work for a personal best.
- Count the number of words read correctly in 30 seconds (words read minus errors). Multiply by two to determine words correct per minute. Record student scores.

b. Partner Reading

During students' daily independent work, have them do Partner Reading.

c. Homework 3

Have students read the story at home. (A reprint of this story is available on a blackline master in *Read Well* Homework.)

STORY 6, SOLO

CHAPTER 6

Free at Last

In the last chapter, who was Harriet helping?[1] What did they want?[2]

Harriet hid Bell, Tom, and the kids. But Tom said, "I hear dogs!"

Harriet said, "If we run in the creek, the dogs can't smell us. The men will not get us."

Tom said, "It will be hard, but we will run fast."

Harriet said, "We will go from farm to farm. We will go from friend to friend."

18

❶ **Summarizing, Identifying—Who** (Harriet was helping Bell and Tom.)

❷ **Summarizing—Goal** (They wanted to be free.)

MAKING CONNECTIONS, RESPONDING, FOCUS ON VOCABULARY

After completing the page, say something like: If you were one of Bell and Tom's kids, how would you have felt?

I think Harriet was very *brave* because she could have gotten caught but she did what she thought was right. Who else do you think was brave? Why?

At last, Harriet said, "Look! We are there."

The kids said, "We are free."

Tom and Bell said, "We are free at last!"

How do you think everyone felt when they got to freedom in the North?[1] No one owned Tom and Bell. No one could take the children away and sell them.[2] Can anyone do that today?[3] Harriet Tubman helped 300 people. I think she was very brave.[4] Who else do you think was brave?[5]

19

❶ **Inferring**

❷ **Teacher Think Aloud**

❸ **Making Connections, Inferring**

❹ **Teacher Think Aloud**

❺ **Responding**

COMPREHENSION BUILDING: ORAL STORY RETELL

- Have students study the pictures, then ask questions and discuss the pictures as indicated in the storybook in light gray text. The circle, square, and triangle provide visual references for the beginning, middle, and end of the story.

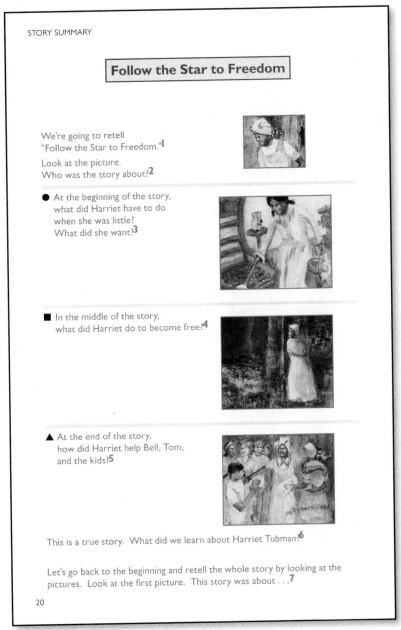

STORY SUMMARY

Follow the Star to Freedom

We're going to retell
"Follow the Star to Freedom."[1]

Look at the picture.
Who was the story about?[2]

● At the beginning of the story,
what did Harriet have to do
when she was little?
What did she want?[3]

■ In the middle of the story,
what did Harriet do to become free?[4]

▲ At the end of the story,
how did Harriet help Bell, Tom,
and the kids?[5]

This is a true story. What did we learn about Harriet Tubman?[6]

Let's go back to the beginning and retell the whole story by looking at the
pictures. Look at the first picture. This story was about . . .[7]

20

❶ **Summarizing, Sequencing**

❷ **Identifying—Who**

❸ **Explaining—Beginning, Identifying—What,
Goal** (She had to scrub the floors and dust. She
worked with the men cutting logs.) (She wanted to
be free.)

❹ **Explaining—Middle, Identifying—Action** (She
ran from the men and dogs. She followed the star
and the moss to freedom.)

❺ **Explaining—End, Action** (At the end of the
story, Harriet helped Bell, Tom, and the kids run
away. They hid in trees. They ran in the creek.
They stayed with Harriet's friends. Harriet helped
Bell, Tom, and the children get to freedom in the
north.)

❻ **Explaining, Describing**

❼ **Summarizing, Sequencing**

STORY COMPREHENSION

Use work pages from the workbook.

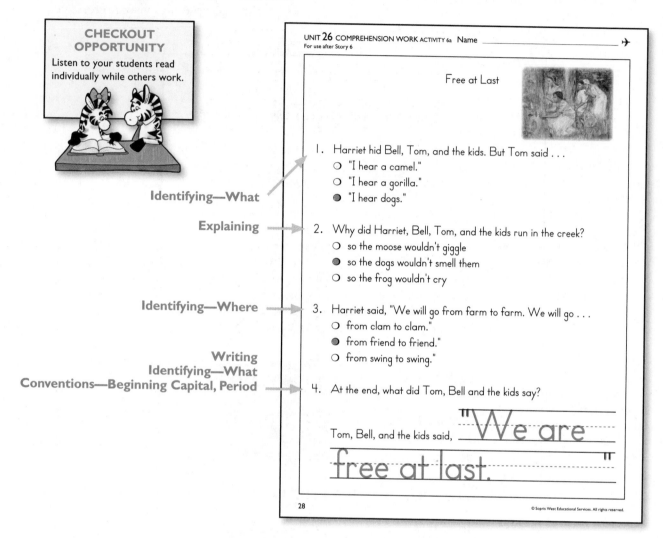

CHECKOUT OPPORTUNITY
Listen to your students read individually while others work.

Identifying—What

Explaining

Identifying—Where

Writing
Identifying—What
Conventions—Beginning Capital, Period

UNIT **26** COMPREHENSION WORK ACTIVITY 6a   Name _____
For use after Story 6

Free at Last

1. Harriet hid Bell, Tom, and the kids. But Tom said . . .
    ○ "I hear a camel."
    ○ "I hear a gorilla."
    ● "I hear dogs."

2. Why did Harriet, Bell, Tom, and the kids run in the creek?
    ○ so the moose wouldn't giggle
    ● so the dogs wouldn't smell them
    ○ so the frog wouldn't cry

3. Harriet said, "We will go from farm to farm. We will go . . .
    ○ from clam to clam."
    ● from friend to friend."
    ○ from swing to swing."

4. At the end, what did Tom, Bell and the kids say?

    Tom, Bell, and the kids said, __"We are__

    __free at last.__

28

PROCEDURES

For each step, demonstrate and guide practice as needed.

1. Multiple Choice—Basic Instructions (Items 1, 2, 3)

Have students fill in the bubble for the correct answer. Periodically, think aloud with students. Discuss the multiple choice options. As appropriate, ask questions like: "Does the first answer make sense?" "Is that what the book said?" "Is the answer completely correct?"

2. Sentence Completion—Basic Instructions (Item 4)

Have students read and complete the sentence, and end it with a period.

RHYMING PATTERNS

Use work pages from the workbook.

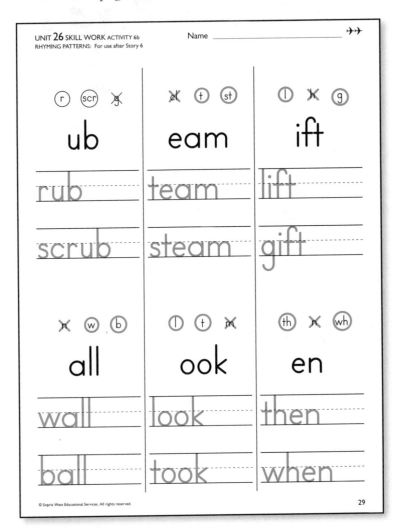

UNIT **26** SKILL WORK ACTIVITY 6b
RHYMING PATTERNS: For use after Story 6

Name _____

(r) (scr) (g̶)

ub

rub

scrub

(c̶) (t) (st)

eam

team

steam

(l) (s̶) (g)

ift

lift

gift

(r̶) (w) (b)

all

wall

ball

(l) (t) (n̶)

ook

look

took

(th) (s̶) (wh)

en

then

when

© Sopris West Educational Services. All rights reserved.

29

CHECKOUT OPPORTUNITY
Listen to your students read individually while others work.

PROCEDURES

Demonstrate and guide practice as needed.

Rhyming Patterns—Basic Instructions

For each box, have students:

- Read the rhyming pattern.
- Circle the two sounds above the rhyming pattern that go with it to make real words.
- Cross out the sound that does not make a real word with the rhyming pattern.
- Write the two rhyming words on the lines provided.

Note: For students who struggle or who lack the English language base to know which are real words, you may wish to identify the two sounds they should circle in each box. Students can then write the pattern words on their own.

Note: There are multiple uses for Decoding Practice 4.
- Use the Sound Review rows in place of Sound Card Practice.
- Use the whole page at the end of the unit for fluency building and/or to informally assess skills.
- Have students complete the page as a partner review.
- Build spelling dictation lessons from the sounds and words on this page.

❶ SOUND REVIEW

❷ ACCURACY AND FLUENCY BUILDING
- Once students are reading the Airplane Columns accurately and confidently, have them work on building their reading rate.
- You might challenge them to read each of the columns in less than five seconds.

❸ TRICKY WORDS

❹ MULTISYLLABIC CHALLENGE WORDS

❺ DAILY STORY READING
See Daily Lesson Planning for story suggestions.

UNIT **26** DECODING PRACTICE 4
(See Daily Lesson Planning for story suggestions.)

1. SOUND REVIEW Demonstrate an appropriate pace. Have students read the sounds in each row.

■	u	g	ee	f	a	l	o	7
✿	Th	b	U	ar	n	c	i	14
♥	m	ea	h	D	-y	sh	e	21

2. ACCURACY/FLUENCY BUILDING For each column, have students say any underlined part, then read each word. Next, have students read the column.

✈	✈✈	✈✈✈	✿	✿✿
dust	hot	ark	<u>rest</u>ed	<u>th</u>e
must	shot	Mark	<u>want</u>ed	<u>th</u>ere
rust	not	bark	<u>need</u>ed	<u>wh</u>ere
crust	got	shark	<u>ask</u>ed	<u>wh</u>en
gust	lot	dark	<u>work</u>ed	<u>th</u>en

3. TRICKY WORDS Have students silently figure out each word, and then read it aloud.

| ☆☆ | because | from | two | couldn't | eggs |
| ☆☆ | friend | No | work | are | The |

4. MULTISYLLABIC CHALLENGE WORDS Have students say each word part, then read the whole word.

| un·self·ish = unselfish | hun·dred = hundred |
| um·brel·la = umbrella | bub·ble gum = bubble gum |

5. DAILY STORY READING

12

End of the Unit

In this section, you will find:

Making Decisions

As you near the end of the unit, you will need to make decisions. Should you administer the Oral Reading Fluency Assessment or should you teach Extra Practice lessons?

Unit 26 Oral Reading Fluency Assessment

The Unit 26 Oral Reading Fluency Assessment is located on page 54 and can also be found in the *Assessment Manual*.

Decoding Diagnosis

If students have difficulty passing the assessment, the Decoding Diagnosis can be used to more accurately diagnose specific problems.

Certificate of Achievement

Celebrate your children's accomplishments.

Extra Practice

Lessons and blackline masters for added decoding practice and independent work are provided for students who need extended practice opportunities.

Making Decisions

ASSESSMENT READINESS

Assess when students are able to easily complete decoding tasks from the beginning of a lesson.

- If you aren't sure whether students are ready for the assessment, give the assessment. Do Extra Practice lessons if needed.
- If students are not ready for the assessment, proceed to Extra Practice lessons. Administer the assessment as soon as students are ready.

GENERAL ASSESSMENT GUIDELINES

- Assess all students.
- Assess each child individually.
- Score student responses on the Student Assessment Record, adhering to the scoring criteria in the *Assessment Manual*. Use a stopwatch to time how long it takes the student to read the oral fluency passage.
- Follow the general instructions at the bottom of each assessment. Record a Strong Pass, a Pass, a Weak Pass, or a No Pass.

ACCELERATION

- If students read with 100% accuracy and exceed the fluency goal, consider shortening units.
- If an individual student reads with greater fluency than others in his or her group, consider regrouping.

INTERVENTION OPTIONS—INDIVIDUALS
(WEAK PASS, NO PASS)

1. Add informal practice throughout the day.
2. Add practice with repeated readings on Solo Stories.
3. Find ways to provide a double dose of *Read Well* instruction.
   - Have the student work in his or her group *and* a lower group.
   - Have an instructional assistant, older student, or parent volunteer preview or review lessons.
   - Have an instructional assistant provide instruction with Extra Practice lessons.
4. Consider placement in a lower group. If one child's fluency scores are significantly lower than the other children in the group, success will be impossible without additional and intensive practice.

INTERVENTION OPTIONS—GROUP (WEAK PASS, NO PASS)

1. Extend the unit with Extra Practice lessons.
2. Consider a Jell-Well Review before moving forward. (See the *Assessment Manual*.)

CERTIFICATE OF ACHIEVEMENT

When students pass the assessment, celebrate with the Certificate of Achievement. Then, set a personal goal. (See *Getting Started*.)

ASSESSING UNPRACTICED READING

Do not have children practice the assessments. The goal of reading instruction is to provide children with the skills to read independently. Repeated readings are an excellent tool for building fluency; however, the end-of-the-unit assessment is designed to assess how well students transfer their skills to unrehearsed passages.

CRITICAL ASSESSMENT

TRICKY WORD WARM-UP

what	legs	shouldn't	friends	two

ORAL READING FLUENCY PASSAGE

Fun in the Sun

★The sun was hot. My friends and I   8

wanted to swim. We asked Dad if he   16

would go with us. Dad said, "I am   24

working until three. Ask Mom about it."   31

Mom said she had to dust, but then   39

she could go. She said, "That will be fun."   48

ORAL READING FLUENCY	Start timing at the ★ Mark errors. Make a single slash in the text (/) at 60 seconds. Have student complete passage. If the student completes the passage in less than 60 seconds, have the student go back to the ★ and continue reading. Make a double slash (//) in the text at 60 seconds.
WCPM	Determine words correct per minute by subtracting errors from words read in 60 seconds.
STRONG PASS	The student scores no more than 2 errors on the first pass through the passage and reads a minimum of 65 or more words correct per minute. Proceed to Unit 27.
PASS	The student scores no more than 2 errors on the first pass through the passage and reads 56 to 64 words correct per minute. Proceed to Unit 27.
WEAK PASS	The student scores no more than 2 errors on the first pass through the passage and reads 48 to 55 words correct per minute. Proceed to Unit 27 with added fluency practice, or provide Extra Practice lessons in Unit 26, and/or provide a Jell-Well Review.
NO PASS	The student scores 3 or more errors on the first pass through the passage and/or reads 47 or fewer words correct per minute. Provide Extra Practice lessons and retest, and/or provide a Jell-Well Review.

Certificate of Achievement

This certifies that

_____ ,

on this _____ day of _____ , ____ ,

has successfully completed

Read Well Unit 26

Sounds Mastered: s, e, ee, m, a, d, th, n, t, w, i, Th, h, c, r, ea, sh, k, -ck, oo, ar, wh, ě, -y (as in "fly"), l, o, b, all, g, f, u

Known Words: By Unit 25, you had learned and practiced 537 words.

New Words Mastered in Unit 26: friend, friends, from, Harriet, worked, working, ark, asked, asking, asks, Ben, bubble gum, but, crust, cut, dust, farm, farms, feel, fun, gust, hundred, logs, must, resting, rug, run, rust, scrub, sell, shot, sun, telling, tells, things, Tom, umbrella, unless, unreal, unselfish, until, us

You can now read 580 words—plus many other words made up of the sounds and patterns you've learned.

Note: Personal and Team Goal Setting forms can be copied from Units 16 and 17, or from *Getting Started.*

Decoding Diagnosis

If students have difficulty passing the Oral Reading Fluency Assessment, the Decoding Diagnosis can be used to more accurately diagnose specific problems. A Decoding Diagnosis is included in the *Assessment Manual* and the Teacher's Guides for Units 19, 23, 26, 28, 30, 34, 36, and 38.

Note: If a student is unable to meet the Oral Reading Fluency goal, he or she may have been misplaced initially, or instruction may have proceeded too fast in the earlier units. If the student makes errors related to one or two skills, you may be able to remediate these skills with intensive work. However, if the student is weak on three or more skills, he or she will need either a careful Jell-Well Review or placement in a lower group.

PROCEDURES FOR ADMINISTERING A DECODING DIAGNOSIS

1. Have the student read from the Decoding Diagnosis. Score on a separate copy.
2. For each subtest, have the student point to and read each item.
3. Make a slash through any item missed and record what the student said above the missed item.

GUIDELINES FOR REMEDIATING SPECIFIC SKILLS

Sounds

- If the student misses only one sound, continue to the next unit but provide additional practice on the difficult sound.
- If the student makes more than one error, consider placing the student in a lower group, providing a Jell-Well Review, or systematically reintroducing one new difficult sound at a time.

Vowel Discrimination

- Have the student practice words that require vowel discrimination. Build lists of words composed of known sounds, with only the vowel changing (e.g., m<u>e</u>t, m<u>a</u>t, m<u>ea</u>t). See the subtest examples.
- Provide additional practice on all the vowel sounds taught to date. Reteach all vowel units, while continuously reviewing all known sounds.

Beginning Quick Sounds

- Have the student practice pairs of rhyming words in which one word begins with a quick sound (e.g., went-<u>d</u>ent, sand-<u>h</u>and).
- Have the student practice lists of words that begin with one quick sound (e.g., had-hid-hard).
- Reteach all units that introduce a quick sound, and review all known sounds.

Blends and Word Endings

- Have the student read lists of words that increase in length, and which include difficult blends and/or word endings (e.g., ack-nack-snack, kitt-kitten).
- Dictate words that build up (e.g., in, ink, rink, drink).

Tricky Words

- Identify the difficult words and increase practice on one difficult word at a time.
- Have the student write any difficult word and use it in a sentence.

SOUNDS

u	F	b	i	l	oo	G	ea
s	a	k	U	r	h	f	e

VOWEL DISCRIMINATION

must	fast	mist	lost	nest
fly	flea	shy	she	shed

BEGINNING QUICK SOUNDS

back	dust	hug	goof	Cass
get	tick	heat	dog	beet

BLENDS AND WORD ENDINGS

thing	bleed	little	asked	shark
hunted	song	scrub	cream	resting

TRICKY WORDS

there	from	worked	about	wanted
isn't	eggs	two	Was	A

• Have students read from a clean copy of the Decoding Diagnosis. Record incorrect responses on another copy.
• Use information from both the Unit 26 Decoding Assessment and the Unit 26 Decoding Diagnosis to identify specific skill deficits.

① SOUNDS

② WORD DICTATION

Follow the procedures below. Use the words in sentences as needed.

us, sun, fun, until

The first word is "us." We're going to count the sounds in "us."
Tell me the first sound. **Hold up one finger.** (/uuu/)
Tell me the next sound. **Hold up two fingers.** (/sss/)
How many sounds are in "us"? (Two)

Tell me the first sound. (/uuu/) Write it.
Tell me the next sound. (/sss/) Write it.
Do Smooth Blending. (/uuusss/) Read the word. (us)

Repeat with "sun," "fun," and "until."

DICTATION
- Demonstrate and guide practice as needed.
- Have students check and correct.

③ SENTENCE COMPLETION
She will go with *us*.
- Have students read the beginning of the sentence with you.
- Dictate the last word "us."
- Have students trace the dotted words and complete the sentence with a period.
- Have students read the sentence.

④ ACCURACY AND FLUENCY BUILDING
Repeat practice on each column, building accuracy first and then fluency.

⑤ TRICKY WORDS
Repeat practice, mixing group and individual turns, independent of your voice.

⑥ DAILY STORY READING
1. First Reading
Have students choral read Fluency Passage 1.

2. Second Reading
- Provide individual turns on sentences. Quietly keep track of errors.
- After reading, practice any difficult words.

3. Repeated Readings
a. Timed Readings

- Have individual students read the passage while other students track the text with their fingers and whisper read. Time individuals for 30 seconds and encourage each student to work for a personal best.
- For each student, determine words correct per minute. Record students' scores.

b. Partner Reading—Checkout Opportunity

- While students are partner reading, listen to individuals read the passage.

Name_____

I. SOUNDS Have students say each sound.

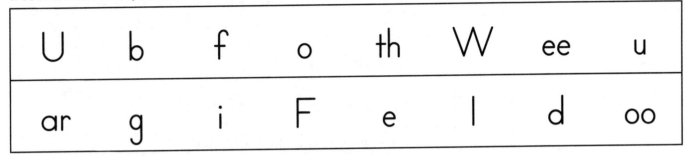

U	b	f	o	th	W	ee	u
ar	g	i	F	e	l	d	oo

2. WORD DICTATION Have students count the sounds in each word, identify and write each sound, and then read the word: "us," "sun," "fun," and "until."

1 _____ 2 _____ 3 _____ 4 _____

3. SENTENCE COMPLETION Have students read the beginning of the sentence. Dictate "us." Have students trace the words and complete the sentence with a period.

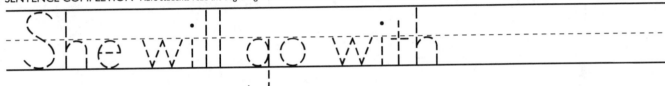

She will go with

4. ACCURACY/FLUENCY BUILDING In each column, have students say any underlined part, then read each word. Next, have students read the column.

♥	♥♥	♥♥♥
but	d<u>o</u>g	<u>a</u>sks
cut	d<u>i</u>g	<u>a</u>sking
dust	d<u>u</u>g	<u>a</u>sked
must	<u>b</u>ug	<u>work</u>ing
rust	b<u>i</u>g	<u>work</u>ed

5. TRICKY WORDS For each word, have students silently figure out the word, then read it aloud.

friends	about	listen	from	legs

6. DAILY STORY READING

Name_____

FLUENCY PASSAGE

> ### Run for Freedom
>
> What did Harriet want? Harriet wanted   6
>
> to be free. What did Harriet do? Harriet ran,   15
>
> and she hid. She ran in the creek. She hid in   26
>
> trees. Where did Harriet go? She ran from   34
>
> farm to farm. At the end, Harriet was free.   43

Have students read the sentences. Time individual students for 30 seconds; mark errors. To determine words correct per minute (wcpm), count words read in 30 seconds, subtract errors, multiply times two, and record on the chart. If student completes the passage in less than 30 seconds, have him or her return to the top and continue reading. (Repeated readings may be completed with older students, assistants, or parents.)

My goal is to read with 0–2 errors. This is what I did:

Reading	1st	2nd	3rd	4th
Errors				
Words/ 30 seconds				
wcpm				

Take-Home Game

Start

Go back 3

Go back 2

Go back 1

End

Materials
Die (or Number Cards 1–6)
Game markers

Game Directions
1. The player rolls one die and then reads the sentence next to the number rolled. (If the player rolls a six, the player reads sentence number six.)
2. The player moves his or her marker the number rolled on the die. (If the player rolls a six, the player moves six spaces.)

Alternative: The player draws a number card instead of using a die. Number cards 1–6. Make at least three cards of each number. Shuffle the cards and place the cards upside down in a draw pile.

1. When Harriet was little, she had to work.

2. Harriet sang as she worked, "Let us go. Let us be free."

3. Ben said, "Feel the moss on the trees."

4. The dogs could smell Harriet, but Harriet ran in the creek.

5. Harriet was free, but Tom was not.

6. Tom and Bell said, "We are free at last!"

❶ SOUNDS

❷ WORD DICTATION

Have students count the sounds in each word with their fingers, identify and write each sound, and then read the word. Use the words in sentences as needed.

hot, he, then, but

The first word is "hot." We're going to count the sounds in "hot."
Tell me the first sound. **Hold up one finger.** (/h/)
Repeat with /ooo/ and /t/.
How many sounds are in "hot"? (Three)

Tell me the first sound. (/h/) Write it.
Repeat with /ooo/ and /t/.
Do Smooth Blending. (/hooot/) Read the word. (hot)

Repeat with "he," "then," and "but."

> **CAUTION**
> Your children may not need Extra Practice. If in doubt, assess students and include Extra Practice only if needed.

HAVE STUDENTS CHECK AND CORRECT.

❸ SENTENCE COMPLETION
Dad had to *dust*.
• Have students read the beginning of the sentence with you.
• Dictate the last word "dust."
• Have students trace the dotted words and complete the sentence with a period.
• Have students read the sentence.

❹ ACCURACY AND FLUENCY BUILDING
Repeat practice on each column, building accuracy first and then fluency.

❺ TRICKY WORDS
Repeat practice, mixing group and individual turns, independent of your voice.

❻ DAILY STORY READING

1. First and Second Readings, Fluency Passage 2a
• Have students choral read the text.
• Provide individual turns on sentences. Quietly keep track of errors.
• After reading, practice any difficult words.

2. First and Second Readings, Fluency Passage 2b
Repeat step one with Fluency Passage 2b.

3. Repeated Readings
   a. Timed Readings

 • Have individual students read either passage 2a or 2b while other students track the text with their fingers and whisper read. Time individuals for 30 seconds and encourage each student to work for a personal best.

• For each student, determine words correct per minute. Record students' scores.

   **b. Partner Reading—
   Checkout Opportunity**

 • While students are partner reading, listen to individuals read a passage.

Name_____

1. SOUNDS Have students say each sound.

u	g	ea	f	a	l	o	b

th	U	ar	wh	i	D	-y	sh

2. WORD DICTATION Have students count the sounds in each word, identify and write each sound, and then read the word: "hot," "he," "then," and "but."

1 _____ 2 _____ 3 _____ 4 _____

3. SENTENCE COMPLETION Have students read the beginning of the sentence. Dictate "dust." Have students trace the words and complete the sentence with a period.

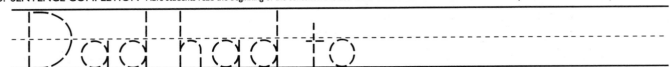

4. ACCURACY/FLUENCY BUILDING In each column, have students say the underlined part, then read each word. Next, have students read the column.

♥	♥♥	♥♥♥
m<u>u</u>st	b<u>u</u>g	<u>work</u>ed
m<u>i</u>st	b<u>i</u>g	<u>ask</u>ed
m<u>a</u>st	d<u>i</u>g	<u>want</u>ed
m<u>e</u>ss	d<u>o</u>g	<u>rest</u>ed
m<u>oo</u>se	d<u>u</u>g	<u>need</u>ed

5. TRICKY WORDS For each word, have students silently figure out the word, then read it aloud.

what	would	friend	could	two

6. DAILY STORY READING

Name_____

FLUENCY PASSAGE A

Harriet Must Be Free

Harriet worked hard. Then she rested in   7

the sun. The man said, "Do not rest." Harriet   16

said, "I must go. I must be free."   24

FLUENCY PASSAGE B

Harriet's Dad

Ben was Harriet's dad. Ben said that   7

Harriet could run. He said, "See the star and   16

feel the moss."   19

My goal is to read with 0–2 errors. This is what I did:

Have students read the sentences. Time individual students for 30 seconds on one passage; mark errors. To determine words correct per minute (wcpm), count words read in 30 seconds, subtract errors, multiply times two, and record on the chart. If student completes the passage in less than 30 seconds, have him or her return to the top and continue reading. (Repeated readings may be completed with older students, assistants, or parents.)

Reading	1st	2nd	3rd	4th
Errors				
Words/ 30 seconds				
wcpm				

❶ STORYBOOK DECODING REVIEW

For each row, mix group and individual turns, independent of your voice.

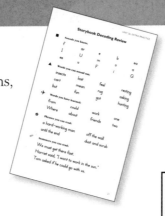

❷ WORD DICTATION

Have students count the sounds in each word with their fingers, identify and write each sound, and then read the word. Use the words in sentences as needed.

if, *Ask*, *but*, *be*

The first word is "if." We're going to count the sounds in "if."
Tell me the first sound. **Hold up one finger.** (/iii/)
Tell me the next sound. **Hold up two fingers.** (/fff/)
How many sounds are in "if"? (Two)

Tell me the first sound. (/iii/) Write it.
Tell me the next sound. (/fff/) Write it.
Do Smooth Blending. (/iiifff/) Read the word. (if)

Repeat with "Ask," "but," and "be."

CAUTION
Your children may not need Extra Practice. If in doubt, assess students and include Extra Practice only if needed.

HAVE STUDENTS CHECK AND CORRECT.

❸ DAILY STORY READING

1. First Reading

Have students choral read Fluency Passage 3.

2. Second Reading

- Provide individual turns on sentences. Quietly keep track of errors.
- After reading, practice any difficult words.

3. Repeated Readings
a. Timed Readings

- Have individual students read the passage while other students track the text with their fingers and whisper read. Time individuals for 30 seconds and encourage each student to work for a personal best.
- For each student, count the number of words read correctly in 30 seconds (words read minus errors). Multiply by two to determine words correct per minute. Record students' scores.

b. Partner Reading—Checkout Opportunity

- Have students partner read. While students are partner reading, listen to individuals read the passage. Work on accuracy or fluency as needed.

Name_____

FLUENCY PASSAGE

Harriet Met Tom and Bell	
Harriet met Tom and Bell. The man	7
wanted to sell Tom and Bell's kids. Harriet	15
had them run in the dark. She had them run	25
from friend to friend. Then Bell said, "Look!	33
We are free. We are free at last."	41

My goal is to read with 0–2 errors. This is what I did:

Have students read the sentences. Time individual students for 30 seconds; mark errors. To determine words correct per minute (wcpm), count words read in 30 seconds, subtract errors, multiply times two, and record on the chart. If student completes the passage in less than 30 seconds, have him or her return to the top and continue reading. (Repeated readings may be completed with older students, assistants, or parents.)

Reading	1st	2nd	3rd	4th
Errors				
Words/ 30 seconds				
wcpm				

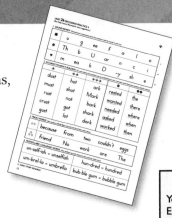

1 DECODING PRACTICE 4 REVIEW

For each row, mix group and individual turns, independent of your voice.

2 WORD DICTATION

Have students count the sounds in each word with their fingers, identify and write each sound, and then read the word. Use the words in sentences as needed.

in, on, if, off

The first word is "in." We're going to count the sounds in "in."
Tell me the first sound. **Hold up one finger.** (/iii/)
Tell me the next sound. **Hold up two fingers.** (/nnn/)
How many sounds are in "in"? (Two)

Tell me the first sound. (/iii/) Write it.
Tell me the next sound. (/nnn/) Write it.
Do Smooth Blending. (/iiinnn/) Read the word. (in)

Repeat with "on," "if," and "off."

> **CAUTION**
>
> Your children may not need Extra Practice. If in doubt, assess students and include Extra Practice only if needed.

> **HAVE STUDENTS CHECK AND CORRECT.**

3 DAILY STORY READING

1. First Reading

Have students choral read Fluency Passage 4.

2. Second Reading

- Provide individual turns on sentences. Quietly keep track of errors.
- After reading, practice any difficult words.

3. Repeated Readings

a. Timed Readings

- Have individual students read the passage while other students track the text with their fingers and whisper read. Time individuals for 30 seconds and encourage each student to work for a personal best.
- For each student, count the number of words read correctly in 30 seconds (words read minus errors). Multiply by two to determine words correct per minute. Record students' scores.

b. Partner Reading—Checkout Opportunity

- Have students partner read. While students are partner reading, listen to individuals read the passage. Work on accuracy or fluency as needed.

Name_____

FLUENCY PASSAGE

Tom's Book	
Tom started telling us about a neat book.	8
We said, "We want to read that book too."	17
Tom said, "I think that would be fun because	26
it is a cool book. It is a book about a big, fat shark."	40
We had fun with that book. The book was	49
about a shark that could bark.	55

My goal is to read with 0–2 errors. This is what I did:

Have students read the sentences. Time individual students for 30 seconds; mark errors. To determine words correct per minute (wcpm), count words read in 30 seconds, subtract errors, multiply times two, and record on the chart. If student completes the passage in less than 30 seconds, have him or her return to the top and continue reading. (Repeated readings may be completed with older students, assistants, or parents.)

Reading	1st	2nd	3rd	4th
Errors				
Words/ 30 seconds				
wcpm				